Chakras for Beginners

The Truth about Balancing Your Chakras and Opening Yourself Up to a World of Increased Health, Wealth and Happiness

Copyright © 2014 by Jessica Jacobs

All rights reserved. No part of this book may be reproduced in any form without permission in writing from the author. Reviewers are able to quote brief passages in reviews.

Disclaimer

This document is geared towards providing exact and reliable information in regards to the topic and issue covered. The publication is sold with the idea that the publisher is not required to render accounting, officially permitted, or otherwise, qualified services. If advice is necessary, legal or professional, a practiced individual in the profession should be ordered.

- *From a Declaration of Principles which was accepted and approved equally by a Committee of the American Bar Association and a Committee of Publishers and Associations.*

In no way is it legal to reproduce, duplicate, or transmit any part of this document in either electronic means or in printed format. Recording of this publication is strictly prohibited and any storage of this document is not allowed unless with written permission from the publisher. All rights reserved.

The information provided herein is stated to be truthful and consistent, in that any liability, in terms of inattention or otherwise, by any usage or abuse of any policies, processes, or directions contained within is the solitary and utter responsibility of the recipient reader. Under no circumstances will any legal responsibility or blame be held against the publisher for any reparation, damages, or monetary loss due to the information herein, either directly or indirectly.

Respective authors own all copyrights not held by the publisher.

The information herein is offered for informational purposes solely, and is universal as so. The presentation of the information is without contract or any type of guarantee assurance.

The trademarks that are used are without any consent, and the publication of the trademark is without permission or backing by the trademark owner. All trademarks and brands within this book are for clarifying purposes only and are the owned by the owners themselves, not affiliated with this document.

About Me

Since opening myself to the spiritual side, I have welcomed a great deal of positivity and happiness into my life and have been living blissfully. There is so much to learn, so many different aspects of life that go completely ignored, and unfortunately the spiritual side is often one of them. When I read about the increasing number of people suffering from depression, stress, and other illnesses, and realized what these annually rising figures entail, I was horrified. While I felt privileged to have peace of mind and soul, I also felt compelled to bring it to the attention of everyone else. In this book, I have compiled my years of research and experience, and I share with you the truth about balancing your chakras.

There's a lot to cover in this book, so let's get right to it.

About This Book

This book starts with the history of the chakras to give you a better understanding of their roots and origins.

After that, you will be introduced to the chakras. What they are, what they do, and where they are in our body.

This introduction will be followed by a chapter that will help you learn about the state of your own chakras by checking certain signs and symptoms.

The rest of the book will chiefly contain different ways, methods, and practices that will help you activate, balance, and align your chakras.

Please note that this book includes two important sections: "How to put this Information into Action" and "Key Takeaways from this Book".

The following table of contents will show you exactly what is covered in this book.

Table of Contents

Introduction 1
Chapter 1. The Origins of Chakras: Chakras through History .. 3
Chapter 2. The Chakras 5
    The Major Chakras 5
        1. The Root Chakra 6
        2. The Sacral Chakra 7
        3. The Solar Plexus Chakra 7
        4. The Heart Chakra 8
        5. The Throat Chakra 8
        6. The Third Eye Chakra 9
        7. The Crown Chakra 9
Chapter 3. Blocked and Out-of-Balance Chakras 11
    The Root Chakra 11
    The Sacral Chakra 13
    The Solar Plexus Chakra 14
    The Heart Chakra 15
    The Throat Chakra 16
    The Third Eye Chakra 17
    The Crown Chakra 18
Chapter 4. Feeding your Chakras with Food 21
    The Root Chakra 21
    The Sacral Chakra 21
    The Solar Plexus 22

 The Heart Chakra 22

 The Throat Chakra 22

 The Third Eye Chakra 23

 The Crown Chakra 23

Chapter 5. Healing your Chakras with Aromatherapy 24

 Aromatherapy 24

  Inhalation 24

  Topical Use 25

  The Root Chakra 25

  The Sacral Chakra 25

  The Solar Plexus Chakra 26

  The Heart Chakra 26

  The Throat Chakra 27

  The Third Eye Chakra 27

  The Crown Chakra 28

 How to Use Essential Oils to Balance Chakras 28

Chapter 6. Balancing your Chakras with Precious Gems and Stones 30

 The Root Chakra 30

 The Sacral Chakra 31

 The Solar Plexus Chakra 31

 The Heart Chakra 31

 The Throat Chakra 32

 The Third Eye Chakra 32

 The Crown Chakra 32

 Balancing the Chakras with Stones 33

The Uses of the Stones 34
Chapter 7. Balancing the Chakras with Color Bathing 37
Chapter 8. Bringing Harmony to your Chakras with Positive Affirmations 39
    The First Chakra or the Root Chakra 39
    The Second Chakra or the Sacral Chakra 39
    The Third Chakra or the Solar Plexus Chakra 39
    The Fourth Chakra or the Heart Chakra 40
    The Fifth Chakra or the Throat Chakra 40
    The Sixth Chakra or the Third Eye Chakra 40
    The Seventh Chakra or the Crown Chakra 40
Chapter 9. Balancing your Chakras with Incantations 41
Chapter 10. Chakra Exercises 43
    The Root Chakra 43
    The Sacral Chakra 44
    The Solar Plexus Chakra 44
    The Heart Chakra 44
    The Throat Chakra 44
    The Third Eye Chakra 45
    The Crown Chakra 45
    Aura Cleansing 45
Chapter 11. Toning your Chakras with Sounds 47
    How to Tone your Chakras with Sounds 47
    The Root Chakra 48
    The Sacral Chakra 48
    The Solar Plexus Chakra 48

- The Heart Chakra 48
- The Throat Chakra 49
- The Third Eye Chakra 49
- The Crown Chakra 49
- The After Exercise 49

Chapter 12. Chakra Mudras 51

- The First Chakra - Root 51
- The Second Chakra - Sacral 51
- The Third Chakra - Solar Plexus 52
- The Fourth Chakra - Heart 52
- The Fifth Chakra - Throat 52
- The Sixth Chakra - Third Eye 52
- The Seventh Chakra - Crown 53

Chapter 13. Aura 54

- Red 54
- Yellow 54
- Pink 55
- Green 55
- Orange 55
- Purple 55
- Blue 56
- Gold 56
- Silver / White 56
- Black 56

Chapter 14. Chakras in Hinduism and Buddhism 57

- Hinduism 57

Buddhism 57
The Differences between Hinduism and Buddhism Relating to Chakras 58

Chapter 15. Opening the Chakras and Meditation 59
    The Root Chakra 60
    The Sacral Chakra 61
    The Navel Chakra 62
    The Heart Chakra 63
    The Throat Chakra 63
    The Third Eye Chakra 64
    The Crown Chakra 65

Chapter 16. Chakras in Relationship 67

Conclusion 70

Key Takeaways from This Book 72

How to Put This Information into Action 73

Resources for Further Reading 74

Preview of *Essential Oils: Learn How to Use the Power of Essential Oils for Aromatherapy, Weight Loss, Stress Relief and Beauty* 75

More Books You Might Like 79

Your Free Bonus 80

Introduction

Life, today, is not as simple as it used to be. There is so much going on, whether we are doing well in our life or otherwise, going up the stairs or down, that we do not even know where to begin our journey to well-being. If we are ever asked, our path to peace and happiness is either related to doing well financially or to eating healthy. Everyone wants to be healthy, wealthy, and wise, but the journey to health, wealth, and wisdom is not merely limited to going to bed and rising early; it goes far beyond that.

It is true that you need to eat healthy to improve your physical health, but you also need to do something to improve your emotional and mental health, the secret to which lies in inner peace. It is inner peace that gives you the strength and fortitude to stand strong in the face of hardships and difficulties. No matter how tough times are, if you are stable internally, there is nothing in the world that you can't do. When there is a lack or excess of something in the body, we develop physical health issues; when there is a lack or excess of a chemical in the brain, we suffer from mental illnesses; and when the chakras are out of balance, the result is a mixture of both mental and physical health problems. And it is for these very reasons that we need to keep our chakras in balance.

The goal of this book is to give an introduction to, increase awareness about, and explain the workings of the chakras in depth. This book is designed in such a way that it will be useful to both beginners and experts alike, whether they need to learn about the chakras from the beginning or just need something to refresh their knowledge.

In this book, I am going to start with the history of the chakras. It is important to know how something came to be, and why it survived through the ages, to actually understand how effective it is and how well it works. After all, the world has seen so much, from the rise and fall of species, like the mighty dinosaurs, to the popularity and doom of things that contribute to well-being. So, if something is able to survive in the age of science and technology, where everything is fully analyzed and scrutinized, then there must be some truth to it, because anything that fails to live up to the mark or makes false claims is immediately discarded. After that, we will get straight into the chakras, starting with the basics, including what chakras are, what effects they have, how they work, why it is important to balance them, and how to balance them. We will also look at the importance of chakras from the perspectives of Buddhism and Hinduism, and the differences between them. You will find tips, tricks, and techniques that will help you balance your chakras and improve your spiritual, physical, and psychological life.

Chapter 1:
The Origins of Chakras: Chakras through History

Chakras can be found in Hindu scriptures and texts dating back over 3,000 - 4,000 years. The exact date of their origin is unknown, but they are often found linked to yoga practices. In the Vedas, the Hindu books of knowledge, the word chakra, spelled as 'cakra', is used. The word 'chakra' means 'wheel', and it is used to describe the wheel of energy or light that is inside us. But there is more to the word than just that; like almost everything else of historical importance its significance is manifold.

There are various explanations for why the word 'chakra' was chosen, and perhaps all of them are true and relevant to some extent. India was invaded by the Aryans, and it is said that when they invaded they came on chariots. In that sense, the word 'chakra' refers to the wheels of their chariots. Another reference it makes could be to the Tantric system; Tantra is an ancient Hindu style of meditation and rituals, and the 'chakra' alludes to the Tantric circle of worshippers. The sun also has a lot of significance for the Hindus. Surya is the name of the sun god, and the sun festival is widely celebrated in India. In that sense the word 'chakra' or 'wheel' refers to the mighty sun rolling in the sky. 'Chakravartin' is a term used in India to describe a universal ruler. The term 'vartin' means 'the one who turns.' Since the ruler is absolute and universal, his 'wheel' rolls everywhere.

After the Vedas come the Upanishads, which are basically the teachings of the Vedas that were passed on from the teachers to their disciples. The Upanishads marked the end of the

Vedas. In the Upanishads that teach about yoga, we can also find chakras being mentioned as the centers of human consciousness.

In 1919, chakras were introduced to the West properly when Arthur Avalon published his book *The Serpent Power*. His book compiled the ancient knowledge and detailed the chakras and their positions in the body. He described how the chakras work, and also shared some practices, including meditation, that could help in healing them. The chakras are positioned in a straight line, leading up from the base of the spine, and each chakra corresponds to a cluster of main nerves. The chakras are divided into two types:

- The Major Chakras
- The Minor Chakras

If a chakra becomes underactive or blocked, it results in other chakras becoming overactive. While you should not try to make a chakra any less active than it is, you should strive to unblock all your chakras. If all the chakras are unblocked, the energy becomes stable and this results in all the chakras being equally active.

In the next chapter, we will discuss what these major and minor chakras are, and what effects they have on our well-being. We will also discuss what the causes of chakra blockage are and how to unblock them.

Chapter 2:
The Chakras

A chakra is an energy point in the body. The chakras spin in their places like wheels, and are connected with each other in a spiral. They regulate and control the flow of energy in our energy system. Every chakra is also related to an endocrine gland and a body part, and controls the functions of that specific gland or organ. It is important to know their positions in the body to understand what body part they correspond to. Negativity is often the factor that slows the spin of the chakras or blocks them altogether. The colors of the chakras are also important, especially if you want to heal, balance, or unblock your chakras using color therapy. Not only does each chakra correspond to a color, but that color also has an effect on it, so the power a chakra has over us also includes the influence of the color to which it corresponds. As we already know, the chakras are divided into two types: major and minor.

The Major Chakras

There are seven major chakras in the body. Each chakra connects us to the life force of the universe. This life force exists naturally in all living things and is known by different names in different philosophies. For instance, in Chinese philosophy, this universal life force is called 'Qi,' or 'Chi.' Its medicinal benefits are not limited to Hinduism, Buddhism, and Jainism either; Chinese medicine has always laid emphasis on the balancing of Qi energy for well-being. The seven major chakras are:

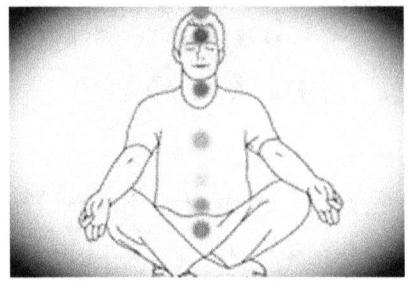

1. The Root Chakra
2. The Sacral Chakra
3. The Solar Plexus Chakra
4. The Heart Chakra
5. The Throat Chakra
6. The Third Eye Chakra
7. The Crown Chakra

As previously mentioned, the chakras start from the base of the spine and go upwards toward the head. You can see how the first chakra, root, goes up through the heart and to the crown. Now, let's get into the details of all the major chakras.

1. *The Root Chakra*

The root chakra is located at the base of the spine. In Sanskrit, its name is 'Muladhara.' It is represented by the color red. Our root chakra is our most physical and primal chakra. Its element is earth and it controls our primal instinct of fight or flight. If it is balanced, we feel confident, secure, grounded, and stable. Our courage, strength, and security depend on our root chakra. Its glandular connection is with the adrenals. The body parts related to the root chakra include legs, hips, kidneys, and spine. When the root chakra is balanced, we feel strong and energetic. Its color also represents self-awareness. It teaches us about the present moment and justifies our existence.

2. *The Sacral Chakra*

The sacral chakra, also known as the sexual chakra, is located just below the navel area. Its Sanskrit name is 'Svadhishthana.' Its corresponding color is orange, and its element is water. It is related to our feelings and sexuality. A balanced sacral chakra leaves us feeling confident and also allows us to accept and experience new things easily. If someone is lively, emotionally stable, can express themselves easily, is passionate, and can enjoy what life has to offer, then they definitely have a stable sacral chakra. The uterus, bowels, sex organs, and prostate are the organs related to it, and its glandular connections are with the testes and the ovaries. It teaches us to respect and honor our fellow human beings.

3. *The Solar Plexus Chakra*

This chakra is located below the chest, about three inches above the navel, between the ribs, and the color that corresponds to it is yellow. 'Manipura' is its Sanskrit name. Our self-esteem, wisdom, and clarity are all regulated by it. How we feel about our life has to do with how balanced our solar plexus chakra is. When balanced, it makes us feel confident, compassionate, and in control. Its element is fire. It has a glandular connection with the adrenals and the pancreas, and the organs it is related to include the stomach, liver, and spleen. It also regulates our outlook on life, and when balanced, makes us see things in a positive light. It teaches us about ourselves, and helps us to accept ourselves.

4. The Heart Chakra

The heart chakra is located at the center of the chest, and its corresponding color is green. 'Anahata' is the Sanskrit name for the heart chakra. It is about love, self-control, and balance in life. Its element is air and its glandular connection is with the thymus, but it is also related to the heart, chest, lungs, and the breasts. When it is balanced, it makes us very loving and compassionate, and also gives us an inner peace that can't be attained in any other way. It is this balance that makes us love and appreciate nature and all things around us. It improves our relationships, makes us understand people better. The balance of this chakra is also important because it makes it easy for us to trust others and to forgive the people who have wronged us. The only thing it teaches about is love.

5. The Throat Chakra

The throat chakra is located in the throat. Its corresponding color is blue, and its Sanskrit name is 'Vishuddha.' Its element is ether, and its glandular connection is with the thyroid and parathyroid. The ears, nose, mouth, neck, teeth, and throat are the body parts associated with it. The throat chakra deals with our self-expression, creativity, communication, knowledge, and health. When this chakra is balanced, we have no problems in communicating and expressing ourselves. If you are an artist, it is especially important to make sure that your throat chakra is stable and unblocked. It teaches us to speak up and get our voice heard.

6. The Third Eye Chakra

The third eye chakra is located in the forehead. Our third eye is our inner eye that gives us insight, and therefore it is located right between and above our outer eyes, in the center of the forehead. In Sanskrit, this chakra is known as 'Ajna.' It is represented by the color indigo. Its element is light, and as it gives us insight into things that we would otherwise not know about, telepathic energy is its other element. The pituitary gland is the main gland associated with it. Other body parts related to it include the eyes, sinuses, base of the skull, and lower head. In its balanced state it allows us to see beyond things, experience things that can't be experienced using the senses, and see the bigger picture. It is also related to intuition, wisdom, inner-vision, and mysticism. The third eye chakra is the chakra that governs perception, knowing, and questioning; use it to question the spiritual side of life. This chakra teaches us to see the bigger picture in different situations of life.

7. The Crown Chakra

The crown chakra is located at the top of the head. Violet is its corresponding color, and its Sanskrit name is 'Sahasrara.' Cosmic energy and thought are its elements. Its glandular connection is with the pineal gland, and the organs it is related to include the skin, upper skull, and brain. It is the chakra that is most stable in visionaries and leaders. When it is stable, it makes us transcendent and brings inner peace and bliss. It is the divine chakra that connects us with God. To be fully spiritual, you need to make sure that your crown chakra is fully open and stable; otherwise, you will not be entirely able to feel the spiritual connection. This chakra teaches us to live our lives mindfully.

These chakras, when working properly, can awaken our spiritual feelings. The spiritual power connects to our mind and body through these chakras. They are associated with our physical, mental, and emotional health. When a chakra is blocked, it results in the over-activity of the other chakras, because the energy in the body remains the same. So if one outlet of energy is blocked, the energy finds its way out through the other chakras. But how do you know if a chakra is underactive, overactive, or blocked?

You can find that out in the next chapter, where we discuss the signs and symptoms of blocked, overactive, and underactive chakras.

Chapter 3. Blocked and Out-of-Balance Chakras

For emotional, physical, and mental well-being, it is important to keep your chakras open and balanced. But first you need to find how well your chakras are performing and whether they are out of balance or not, blocked or open. If a chakra is blocked, the extra energy finds its way out through the other chakras, and destabilizes your life. For instance, if one of the chakras is blocked and the energy is directed to the second chakra, the sacral chakra, it will make you emotionally unstable. In this chapter, we will discuss how a blocked chakra affects you, and what happens when a chakra is underactive or overactive. Having an overactive chakra is not a good thing either, because inner peace comes from balance, not from an excess of energy. If you find that your chakras are overactive, you do not need to work on making them any less active than they are; instead, you need to open and improve the blocked or underactive chakras, so that balance can be restored. Another reason to keep your chakras in balance is to avoid the health issues they can cause when not in balance.

The Root Chakra
Balanced: In its balanced state the root chakra establishes high physical energy, keeps us grounded and healthy, and improves our self-mastery. It makes it easy for us to connect with others, our family, friends, and the world. It is important to have this chakra unblocked to be able to live your life fully, not giving way to paranoia and distrust of others, and to feel light and free.

Blocked: If the first seven years of your life were difficult or challenging, and you were not loved like you should have been, then your root chakra is damaged. A blocked root chakra manifests itself by decreasing your self-esteem, making you fearful of others and the world, destabilizing your emotional stability by making you emotionally needy and paranoid, and often sets you on a path of self-destructive behavior. It makes you feel like you need to defend yourself against everything. It also takes your focus away so you can't concentrate on work and end up procrastinating.

Underactive: When the root chakra is underactive it leaves you feeling nervous and afraid, and unwelcome in social situations.

Overactive: When it is overactive, it makes you become obsessed with worldly things. It makes you greedy, overly materialistic, self-centered, and a bully. You become so obsessed with things that you do not welcome change in your life and do your best to oppose it.

Health Issues: The health issues caused by an unbalanced or blocked root chakra result in physical problems relating to the immune system, reproductive organs, feet, legs, rectum, tailbone, and prostate gland. It causes diseases and problems like constipation, sciatica, arthritis, pain in the knees, lower back, and joints, as well as anorexia, obesity, and eating disorders. The toll it takes is not merely physical but manifests in emotional issues as well. The emotional issues it causes are related to our basic needs, including our need for money, food, safety, and shelter.

The Sacral Chakra

Balanced: The sacral chakra has to do with our feelings and sexuality. It helps us understand the different flavors of the world and the power of opposites, like the opposite ends of positivity and negativity, man and woman, etc. It is also related to creativity and emotions. When it is balanced, it makes it easy for us to express ourselves, trust others, and maximize our creativity. It is important to keep this chakra balanced so that we can experience and enjoy the things that life has to offer, take risks and not feel guilty about things that we do.

Blocked: A blocked sacral chakra results in suppression of our feelings, obsessive and compulsive behavior, oversensitivity, guilt, and even impotence. It takes away the passion from our life, and can make us feel betrayed and prone to addictions.

Underactive: When the sacral chakra is underactive, our emotions are suppressed. They are not completely gone but they are greatly reduced. As human beings, we need to show others how we feel about them, how grateful or upset we are for things they have done, etc., and that can't happen when we do not show any emotions at all.

Overactive: If this chakra is overactive, our emotions are more abundant than they need to be. The balance is gone and we find that we have become too sensitive and emotional. We lose control of our impulses, start manipulating others for our own gain, engage in inappropriate sexual activity, and end up being fantasists.

Health Issues: The health issues caused by the blockage or imbalance of the sacral chakra manifest physically in urinary and bladder problems, dysfunction of kidneys, problems in the large intestines, sexual problems, and problems in the pelvic area, hips, or pain in the lower back. Sexual dysfunction, sciatica, and lack of flexibility are also attributed to its imbalance. The emotional issues caused by it include difficulty making commitments, relationship issues, and problems with sexuality.

The Solar Plexus Chakra

Balanced: The solar plexus chakra has a lot to do with harmony, and is affected by how the chakras above and below it perform. If they are not well-balanced, this chakra will be thrown off balance too, and if they are in perfect harmony, this chakra will do better as well. In its balanced state, it increases our self-respect, confidence, spontaneity, personal power, self-control, self-esteem, and self-honoring, along with our warmth, understanding, and intellect. It makes us feel that we are the ones in control.

Blocked: When it is blocked, it makes us lose courage and confidence easily. Our self-esteem is decreased and we become overly sensitive to criticism, even if it is constructive. It leaves us feeling insecure, and we become afraid of being lonely. We start thinking too much about what other people think, we worry more than we should, and we lose the direction in our life. It makes us feel like we are victims, which can make us angry and frustrated.

Underactive: When it is underactive, we become indecisive and can't really tell what we want. We let others lead us instead of being leaders ourselves, and do not raise our voice for what we want.

Overactive: When this chakra is overactive, we find ourselves angry and lose our temper easily. We become demanding and controlling, and we start judging others because we believe that we are superior to everyone else. It also makes us very aggressive and domineering.

Health Issues: The physical issues caused by it include anxiety, nervousness, high blood pressure, diabetes, ulcers in the stomach, liver problems, chronic fatigue, and problems with the colon, pancreas, and gallbladder, as well as problems of the digestive system. It also causes muscle cramps, and decreases energy. It makes us emotionally fragile, overly concerned with our looks, afraid of being rejected, and overly critical of ourselves.

The Heart Chakra

Balanced: The heart chakra is in the center, or middle, of all the chakras. It is also heavily influenced by, and influences, the workings of other chakras. The heart chakra has to do with love and forgiveness. When it is balanced, it makes us compassionate, loving, friendly, and forgiving. It improves our relationships with others. Just like a healthy pair of lungs makes it easy for us to breathe, a balanced heart chakra allows us to love unconditionally. It allows us to feel joy, to love, and to forgive. In short, our ability to love, forgive, trust, and get inner peace depends on it.

Blocked: When the heart chakra is blocked, it gives way to self-pity. We fear rejection, feel like we are not worthy of receiving love from others, and become jealous, lonely, and bitter. It also takes away our compassion, makes us inhumane, and leads to immoral behavior.

Underactive: An underactive heart chakra takes away our empathy and makes us cold and hard. It disconnects us from others and we become more distant.

Overactive: When the heart chakra is overactive, we become selfish and start doing things for our own gain, and even our love has ulterior motives.

Health Issues: Imbalance or blockage of the heart chakra manifests in physical problems such as lung and heart diseases, asthma, diseases of the lymphatic system and breasts, and pain in the arms, wrists, upper back and lower back, as well as chest pains and shortness of breath. The emotional toll it takes makes us bitter, jealous, and angry, and leaves us feeling abandoned. Sometimes, people with a blocked heart chakra can end up driving people away from themselves.

The Throat Chakra

Balanced: An important part of leading a happy and successful life lies in being able to express ourselves, whether it is to show gratitude to others for things they have done, to appreciate or motivate others, or to show them that we care. And the capacity for self-expression is especially important for artists, be they writers, painters, illustrators, actors, etc. It is important to be able to express what you want and what you feel, and expression is governed by the throat chakra. It helps us communicate well. When it is balanced, we have a strong voice and are able to voice our opinions in support of what we believe in. It makes it easy for us to manage our stress and to meditate. We are good listeners when it is balanced.

Blocked: If the throat chakra is blocked, it holds us back from expressing ourselves. For writers, it often manifests itself in the form of writer's block, and I, just like any other writer, know how big of a setback that is and how much stress it brings. It is not just limited to writers, though; any form of expression, artistic or dramatic, gets suppressed. It makes communication really difficult. People with a blocked throat chakra tend to hold inconsistent and contradictory views. It also leads to dishonesty and suppression of feelings. Our own voice becomes so weak that we find it difficult to understand ourselves.

Underactive: People who have an underactive throat chakra tend to be shy and introverted. They don't speak when they should.

Overactive: When the throat chakra is overactive, people end up becoming too dramatic. They become controlling, possessive, and domineering. They speak up even when they do not need to, drive others away, and are not able to listen to what others have to say. It leads to arrogance and self-righteousness.

Health Issues: Lack of harmony and an imbalance of the throat chakra results in physical problems, such as fevers and facial problems including problems with the tongue, cheeks, lips, and chin. It also causes thyroid issues, laryngitis, ear infections, sore throat, and ulcers. Problems of the esophagus, cervical spine, neck, throat, and voice are also caused by it. The emotional imbalances it causes include problems with communicating verbally or in writing, difficulty expressing yourself, and a feeling that you are losing control or can't control yourself.

The Third Eye Chakra
Balanced: When the third eye chakra is balanced, we are open to the spiritual world. It goes beyond the ordinary and sensory stuff, and allows us to see, feel, and experience the divine. It improves our insight and instincts. We may experience unusual phenomena, be highly intuitive, and become

charismatic when it is balanced. It gives us clarity, improves our focus, and we can tell the difference between the real and the surreal. It is also associated with wisdom.

Blocked: When this chakra is blocked the result is usually depression. It makes us timid and afraid of success, mentally rigid, and prone to schizophrenia. The blockage of the third eye chakra also results in delusions, memory loss, and a lack of imagination. Signs of its blockage also include zoning out, losing focus, inability to keep up with a conversation, and worrying incessantly. It takes away your ability to learn from your mistakes, or those of others.

Underactive: If this chakra is underactive, you are not able to decide and think for yourself. You need help from, and rely on, others to guide you or lead you. People with an underactive third eye chakra are often confused.

Overactive: When the third eye chakra is overactive, people lose focus and fail to see the difference between what is real and what is unreal. They may start fantasizing or hallucinating.

Health Issues: The physical issues caused by it include seizures, headaches, blurred vision, issues of the sinuses, eyestrain, and even hearing loss. The emotional issues caused by it include volatility, mood swings, day-dreaming, neurological problems, excessive imagination, and living in a world of fantasies.

The Crown Chakra

Balanced: When the crown chakra is fully balanced, we are able to live in the present. We believe in ourselves and trust our own wisdom and instincts. It connects us to our God, and to the world. In essence, it truly helps us become one with the world. The spiritual energy flows through us when the crown chakra is balanced. It makes us feel at peace with ourselves, makes us transcendent, and even makes our personality more magnetic. It is in this state that miracles can be achieved.

Blocked: When this chakra is blocked, it leads to confusion, depression, and senility. It blocks inspiration and spiritual energy as well. We feel lost and don't know where we belong. It also leads to people feeling disassociated with their bodies.

Underactive: When it is underactive, we fail to connect with our spiritual side. It makes us rigid.

Overactive: The over-activity of the crown chakra leads people to over-intellectualizing and becoming overly spiritual. They get so obsessed with the spiritual side of things that they ignore the worldly side, including their own physical and bodily needs. It causes manic depressive and psychotic episodes, and also causes frustration.

Health Issues: The health issues that are caused by an out-of-balance crown chakra include depression, sensitivity to light, sound, and environment, mental disorders, skin problems, migraines, tumors, amnesia, and even coma. The emotional impact of the imbalance results in an exaggerated sense of power, confusion, and a fear of becoming alienated.

Note: In this chapter, we went into detail about what happens when a chakra is out of balance, underactive, or overactive. Remember that the key lies in the peace and harmony of the chakras, and attaining that is our goal. An overactive or an underactive chakra is just about as harmful as a blocked chakra. All the states of the chakras are directly linked, in that a blocked chakra or an underactive chakra makes other chakras overactive. An overactive chakra can result in other chakras becoming underactive or getting blocked altogether. So, if you notice any of the signs and symptoms of a blocked, an overactive, or an underactive chakra in yourself, then know that you need to correct them. It is important to restore balance to the chakras to lead a happy, successful, peaceful, and blissful life. There are various ways to correct the chakras, and that is exactly what I will tell you about in the next chapters.

Chapter 4. Feeding your Chakras with Food

Since chakras affect us on many different levels, including physical, emotional, mental, and psychological, healing is required on different levels too. To heal, balance, and align your chakras, and to restore harmony to them, you need to fix them on different levels. As they say, you are what you eat. In part, that can be attributed to the chakras. What you eat feeds your chakras, and when they are out of balance, there are certain things that you can eat to make them strong, and to harmonize and realign them. If you are wondering why the foods are important, you will be surprised to know that food not only fuels the body but also fuels the chakras. Following is what you need to eat in order to fix or balance each chakra.

The Root Chakra
Since this chakra is at the root of all chakras, it is naturally healed chiefly by eating root foods. The vegetables that you can eat to heal it include: beets, carrots, garlic, onions, parsnips, and potatoes. Proteins are also recommended for feeding this chakra. They include: beans, eggs, meats, peanut butter, soy products, and tofu. Since the chakras have their roots in Indian tradition, it is only natural that spices are also important parts of their food. For the root chakra, they include: chives, cayenne, horseradish, pepper, and paprika.

The Sacral Chakra
The foods for the sacral chakra are chiefly sweet fruits and nuts. You can feed your sacral chakra by eating coconuts,

melons, mangoes, passion fruits, and strawberries. Honey, almonds, and walnuts are all power-packed and good fuels for the chakras. The spices for feeding this chakra include: carob, caraway seeds, cinnamon, sesame seeds, sweet paprika, and vanilla.

The Solar Plexus
The solar plexus chakra relies on grains, dairy, and spices for strength. The grains and granola that you can feed it with include: breads, cereals, flax seeds, pasta, and sunflower seeds. Cheese, milk, and yoghurt are the dairy products that it can be fed with, while the spices you can feed it with include: cumin, chamomile, fennel, spearmint, and peppermint.

The Heart Chakra
The central chakra, the heart chakra, can be fed by liquids, leaves, and leafy vegetables. The leafy vegetables to feed it with are broccoli, cabbage, cauliflower, celery, kale, spinach, and dandelion. The spices and herbs that it can be fed with include basil, cilantro, parsley, sage, and thyme. You can also feed it with a healthy brew of green tea leaves.

The Throat Chakra
The throat chakra, the chakra that gives you your voice, also relies on liquids and fruits for power. Lemons, limes, grapefruits, and kiwis are the fruits it should be fed with, as well as apples, apricots, pears, peaches, and plums. The spices for the throat chakra include salt and lemongrass, and the liquids include water, fruit juices, and herbal teas as well as green tea.

The Third Eye Chakra
The third eye chakra relies on dark colored berries and drinks for strength. The berries include: blueberries, blackberries, red grapes, and raspberries, and the spices it can be fed with include mugwort, poppy seeds, and lavender. It can also be fed with grape juice or red wine.

The Crown Chakra
The crown chakra is less physical and more divine, and its strength does not come from food. To feed it, you need clear, fresh air. Go out in the morning to take in all the fresh air, or meditate. You can also burn incense sticks made from copal, myrrh, juniper, frankincense, and sage.

When your chakras are fed, you are filled with an internal satisfaction. It is similar to the satisfaction you get when you fill your stomach after being hungry for a long time. It is inherent and subtle, so some people might not be able to tell the difference, but when the chakras are fed, they don't make you feel it because they return to their normal, peaceful, and harmonic state.

Chapter 5. Healing your Chakras with Aromatherapy

Aromatherapy is an alternative medicine, an age-old technique which has been practiced since ancient times. It makes use of the oils extracted from plants and flowers for treating medical conditions, relaxing, and healing the body. It is also used to heal damaged chakras. Aromatherapy is still popular today, chiefly because it is effective and affordable. Not much is required for it; usually you just need the essential oils and something to measure them. Measuring instruments can be ignored if your essential oil bottle comes with a dropper tip and you know how many drops of oil you need. The best thing about aromatherapy is that the oils are organic and chemical-free, so there are no pesticides, insecticides, or fungicides in them, and they are not harmful. This approach is holistic, and along with healing, it also reduces stress and improves overall health.

Aromatherapy

There are two basic ways in which you can use the oils:

- Inhalation
- Topical Use

Inhalation
Inhaling an essential oil is perhaps the most effective method. When you inhale an oil, it goes straight into your body through your mouth or nose. The resulting effect is immediate relief.

Topical Use

When used topically, the oil is applied directly onto the skin. There is some inhalation in this case too, but the main focus remains on the topical application. The effectiveness of each method depends on the ailment.

You can either burn an incense stick or use an essential oil for each chakra. If you find that an essential oil has a smell too strong for you, as may be the case with many essential oils, you can mix it with a carrier oil. The smells are strong because the oils are very pure, but mixing them with a carrier oil like almond oil can make them bearable. The following is a list of essential oils that you can use to heal the chakras:

The Root Chakra

The oils that can be used to heal the root chakra are:

- Benzoin essence oil
- Clematis essence oil
- Cedar-wood essence oil
- Corn essence oil
- Frankincense essence oil
- Lavender essence oil
- Myrrh essence oil
- Patchouli essence oil
- Rosemary essence oil
- Sandalwood essence oil
- Yang-ylang essence oil

The Sacral Chakra

The oils that can be used to heal the sacral chakra are:

- Hibiscus essence oil
- Indian Paintbrush essence oil
- Jasmine essence oil
- Lady's Slipper essence oil
- Melissa essence oil
- Neroli essence oil
- Orange essence oil
- Rose essence oil
- Sandalwood essence oil

The Solar Plexus Chakra

The oils that can be used to heal the solar plexus chakra are:

- Bergamot essence oil
- Chamomile essence oil
- Cinnamon essence oil
- Lemon juniper essence oil
- Marjoram essence oil
- Peppermint essence oil
- Petitgrain essence oil
- Vetiver essence oil
- Yarrow essence oil
- Ylang-ylang essence oil

The Heart Chakra

The oils that can be used to heal the heart chakra are:

- Bergamot essence oil
- Eucalyptus essence oil
- Holly essence oil
- Jasmine essence oil

- Melissa essence oil
- Pine essence oil
- Poppy essence oil
- Rose essence oil
- Rosewood essence oil
- Watermelon essence oil

The Throat Chakra
The oils that can be used to heal the throat chakra are:

- Blue essence oil
- Chamomile essence oil
- Cosmos essence oil
- Geranium essence oil
- Hyssop essence oil
- Larch essence oil
- Lemongrass essence oil
- Myrrh essence oil
- Sage essence oil
- Trumpet vine essence oil

The Third Eye Chakra
The oils that can be used to heal the third eye chakra are:

- Clary Sage essence oil
- Elemi essence oil
- Frankincense essence oil
- Geranium essence oil
- Hyacinth essence oil
- Lavender essence oil
- Madia essence oil

- Patchouli essence oil
- Peppermint essence oil
- Queen Anne's Lace essence oil
- Rose essence oil
- Rosemary essence oil
- Spruce essence oil
- Violet essence oil
- Wild Oat essence oil

The Crown Chakra
The oils that can be used to heal the crown chakra are:

- Angelica essence oil
- Benzoin essence oil
- Frankincense essence oil
- Jasmine essence oil
- Lavender essence oil
- Lotus essence oil
- Myrrh essence oil
- Neroli essence oil
- Rosewood essence oil
- Star Tulip essence oil
- St. John's Wort essence oil
- Sandalwood essence oil

How to Use Essential Oils to Balance Chakras

The simplest and the most direct way to use an essential oil to heal your chakra is to take a drop or two of the oil and rub it directly on the skin above the chakra that you want to heal. So if you want to heal your throat chakra, you will rub the drops of oil directly on your throat.

If, for some reason, you can't or do not want to rub the oil directly onto your skin, then there is another easy way to do it, and it combines both the inhalation and topical methods. Rub the drops of oil on your palms and then start waving your hands. The chakras are all about balance, and here you can restore balance to them. The positive and negative energies need to be balanced properly, so first wave your hands in an anti-clockwise direction to get rid of all the negative energies. Then wave your hands in a clockwise direction to restore balance to the positive energies.

The proper method for inhalation includes the use of an oil diffuser. The oil diffuser consists of a small stand over which there is a small bowl. There is room to place a small candle underneath the bowl. To use it, you have to add some water to the bowl, and then add a few drop of the essential oil, and light the candle underneath it. The fire from the candle will heat the bowl, and as the temperature of the water increases, the essence of the oil begins to diffuse in the air. Take deep breaths, inhale, and relax as the therapy heals your chakras.

The oils have medicinal properties, and you could be allergic to some of them, so make sure that you do not ingest any oil or come in contact with one that you are allergic to. Since there are many different oils for each chakra, if you are allergic to one you can use another oil that you are not allergic to.

Chapter 6. Balancing your Chakras with Precious Gems and Stones

Precious gems and stones are known for their healing powers. They are widely worn as jewelry in the form of rings, earrings, and necklaces. Wands containing these stones are used to open blocked chakras. These naturally occurring gems and stones have an energy of their own which helps balance the energy of the chakras. As I said earlier, each chakra has a color corresponding to it, so the gems that are used for these chakras are also of the same colors. The following is a list of the crystals used for healing each chakra:

The Root Chakra
The stones, gems, and crystals used to heal the root chakra include:

- Black Obsidian
- Black Tourmaline
- Blood Stone
- Garnet
- Hematite
- Onyx
- Red Zincite
- Ruby
- Tiger Eye
- Smoky Quartz

The Sacral Chakra
The stones, gems, and crystals used to heal the sacral chakra include:

- Blue-green Turquoise
- Blue-green Fluorite
- Carnelian
- Citrine
- Orange Calcite
- Vanadinite

The Solar Plexus Chakra
The stones, gems, and crystals used to heal the solar plexus chakra include:

- Citrine
- Golden Calcite
- Yellow Citrine
- Yellow Calcite
- Yellow Jasper

The Heart Chakra
The stones, gems, and crystals used to heal the heart chakra include:

- Aventurine
- Green Aventurine
- Jade
- Malachite
- Pink Tourmaline
- Rose Quartz

- Rubellite Tourmaline
- Watermelon Tourmaline

The Throat Chakra

The stones, gems, and crystals used to heal the throat chakra include:

- Angelite
- Blue Calcite
- Blue Kyanite
- Blue Turquoise
- Lapis Lazuli
- Sodalite
- Turquoise

The Third Eye Chakra

The stones, gems, and crystals used to heal the third eye chakra include:

- Amethyst
- Azurite
- Lapis Lazuli
- Purple Apatite
- Sapphire
- Sugilite or Lavulite

The Crown Chakra

The stones, gems, and crystals used to heal the crown chakra include:

- Amethyst
- Clear Quartz
- Diamond
- White Calcite
- White Topaz

To balance your chakras, you should find the respective gem or stone and wear it as a ring, earring, in a necklace, or just carry it around. The stones not only have energies but are also very beautiful. When used as a decoration in a room, they can fill the room with positive energy. You can sometimes feel the energy when you pick the stone up, but if that does not happen then that does not mean that the stone is ineffective. Sometimes it takes time to feel the power of the stone.

Balancing the Chakras with Stones

There is a simple exercise that you can perform to balance your chakras using stones. To properly balance all the chakras, it is recommended that you have a stone for each chakra at hand.

Lie down on a comfortable surface and relax. Calm down and focus on your breathing. Pick up a White Topaz (or any other stone for the crown chakra) and place it on your head, right above the crown. Leave it there for a few minutes and feel the energy heal and balance the chakra. Then after 3-5 minutes, pick up an amethyst or Lapis Lazuli and place it in the center of your forehead for the third eye chakra. Give it a few minutes to set in and take effect. Repeat this process for each chakra by placing stones on the relevant body areas. If a stone falls off or rolls down, do not bother picking it up. Continue to focus, close your eyes, and visualize the stones transferring their energy into you, healing and balancing your chakras, making you feel whole again.

This exercise can be done in as little as 21 minutes. Once done, remove the stones and store them somewhere safe. Repeat the exercise as frequently as needed.

The Uses of the Stones

Not all the stones possess the same properties, and in order to use them properly, you need to know what each of them does.

Amber is used for opening and cleaning the solar plexus chakra.

Amethyst is used for activating the crown chakra, or opening it when it is blocked.

Celestite can be used to clear any chakra and to perfect it.

Citrine serves many purposes. It is used to balance and align all the chakras. It opens and activates the sacral and solar plexus chakras, stimulates the crown chakra, and gives energy to the root chakra.

To activate the crown chakra, *copal* is used.

Bloodstone (heliotrope) is used to activate and balance the root chakra, solar plexus chakra, throat chakra, and heart chakra.

Black obsidian is beneficial to the root chakra.

Black tourmaline removes the negativity from all chakras, and is especially used to restore balance to the root chakra.

Carnelian agate is used for the first four chakras, and also boosts creativity, physical energy, and compassion.

Chrysoprase can be used to activate the heart chakra and to align the others.

Deep pink tourmaline is used for improving connections of the heart chakra and for stimulating the root chakra.

Garnet is used to speed up the healing of the body, to drive away negative energy from the chakras, and to stimulate the root chakra.

Green aventurine is used in clearing, activating, and protecting the heart chakra.

Green fluorite is used to renew all the chakras or to cleanse them.

Green tourmaline is beneficial for the heart chakra.

Hematite is used for cleaning the root chakra. When the root chakra is overactive, it can be used to close it.

Herkimer diamond activates the crown chakra.

Kyanite is used to align all seven chakras automatically. When the chakras are blocked, it can be used to open them.

Lapis lazuli is used for activating the throat and third eye chakras, and also to clear them.

Malachite is used to stimulate the heart and throat chakras.

Moldavite is beneficial to the throat, third eye, and crown chakras.

Moonstone is used to clear negative energies from all the chakras.

Pink kunzite is used for the alignment and balancing of all the chakras; it is also used to activate the heart chakra.

Quartz crystal balances the heart chakra and heals its wounds. It also activates the crown chakra and enhances the clarity of consciousness. It is also used for opening all the chakras.

Rose quartz is used to balance the energies of all the chakras.

Smoky quartz is beneficial to the root chakra.

Tiger eye promotes and enhances intuition and psychic abilities at the solar plexus chakra and the third eye chakra respectively.

Turquoise, when used for the throat chakra, improves communication.

Watermelon tourmaline is extremely beneficial in activating the heart chakra.

White calcite is used to stimulate all the chakras, and is ideal for the crown chakra.

Chapter 7. Balancing the Chakras with Color Bathing

Once the chakras are healed and restored with food, precious stones, and aromatherapy, you can move on to color bathing to further enhance them, or just to keep them in balance and sync. The color bathing method is as follows:

Start by filling a bathtub with water, and make sure that the temperature of the water is neither too hot nor too cold. It should be moderate so that you do not get uncomfortable in it. Sit in an easy and relaxed position in the tub, and take a long, deep, breath. As with all meditative exercises, focus on your breathing and slow it down by inhaling through the nose and exhaling through the mouth. Take three deep breaths in the same way, and then picture a white, holy light, the love from the universe, coming towards you. Once it reaches you, picture it spinning around you in an anti-clockwise direction. It should start from your feet and gradually move up towards your heard or the crown chakra.

After that, visualize a purple light of energy moving around you. It should start from your head, circling around you in an anti-clockwise direction, and move towards your feet slowly. Once it reaches your feet, it returns to the crown chakra at the same speed it went down. If your chakras are blocked, you will have trouble with this, but with practice, patience, and persistence, you can master it. You can also visualize it moving in a clockwise motion, if anti-clockwise motion is difficult for you to visualize.

Once that is done, imagine an indigo light. This is the light for your third eye chakra. Again, think of this light circling you in an anti-clockwise motion, starting from your head and moving towards your feet slowly, going up and down, over and again.

Then visualize a blue light for the throat chakra, starting from your head and moving toward the feet. Slowly, swirling around you, this light should move from your head to your toes, back to your head, and to the toes again. Keep visualizing until you get used to the light.

Then picture a green light for the heart chakra. The color of the light energy should be the one that corresponds to the chakra. The light should move either in a clockwise or in an anti-clockwise direction, from your head to your toes, from your toes to your head, slowly and gently caressing you, healing you, fixing you, and restoring balance.

The light for the solar plexus chakra will be yellow. Again, the direction of swirling should be the one that is easy for you to visualize. Imagine it going up and down your body slowly, and when it feels like it is in control and is automatically going up and down slowly, you can move on to the base.

The root chakra has a red light. This is the chakra that grounds you. Imagine this light going up and down, just like the previous lights, slowly and gently, swirling around you, moving gently, bringing harmony to your root chakra.

You can continue this exercise for as long as you want, as it not only heals but also serves meditative purposes.

Chapter 8. Bringing Harmony to your Chakras with Positive Affirmations

Positive affirmations are a crucial and basic part of positive thinking. They are used in meditation and stress management techniques to help clear the mind and increase focus. They also heal and balance chakras and increase their positive energy. The affirmations are simple and easy to remember, and you can either write them down and place them somewhere where you can read them easily, or memorize them and repeat them whenever you are comfortable and want to harmonize your chakras.

The First Chakra or the Root Chakra
Affirmation: "I am connected to Mother Earth and feel the security of being grounded in the moment. I deserve the best life has to offer; all my needs are being met. My body is important to me and I nurture it constantly."

The Second Chakra or the Sacral Chakra
Affirmation: "I trust that all is well. Creativity is flowing freely through me."

The Third Chakra or the Solar Plexus Chakra
Affirmation: "I own my personal power. I accept myself exactly for who I am."

The Fourth Chakra or the Heart Chakra
Affirmation: "I am lovable. I love unconditionally. I love myself for who I am. Other people deserve my compassion."

The Fifth Chakra or the Throat Chakra
Affirmation: "I am speaking my truth. What I say is worthy of being listened to. I listen to and acknowledge the needs and wants of others."

The Sixth Chakra or the Third Eye Chakra
Affirmation: "The answers to all my questions lie within me. Imagination sparks my creativity. I trust my intuition."

The Seventh Chakra or the Crown Chakra
Affirmation: "I am who I am and glory in that. I attune with my higher power. I am a unique, loving, radiant being."

Chapter 9. Balancing your Chakras with Incantations

Another easy way to balance your chakras is with incantations. Just like positive affirmations, these incantations are also packed with energy. What we tell ourselves, what we believe, has the power to shape our lives. Just like being negative attracts negative energies, being positive attracts positive energies. When we repeat these incantations, when we tell ourselves these things, the energies balance out and strengthen us.

The exercise for the incantations is very simple. The only thing you need is a quiet and meditative environment. You can either sit, lie down, or stand, as you feel comfortable, for this exercise. Standing in front of the window, taking in the sun, is also a good position for this, as sun is a supreme source for charging all the chakras. Seven of the incantations are for each of the major chakras, while the rest are for energy, aura, and balance. When you inhale, repeat the part of the sentence that is highlighted, and repeat the other part when you exhale. Inhale and exhale very slowly, each inhalation lasting for five seconds, and each exhalation also lasting for five seconds. Our focus and concentration improves when we are breathing slowly. This technique combines the power of positive thinking and meditation with the incantations to balance the chakras.

My energy is free of blockages

My root chakra is deeply grounded

My sacral chakra juices are creative and bold

My solar plexus feels mellow and calm

My heart is filled with love

My throat speaks the truth

My third eye intuits inner knowledge

My crown chakra projects inspiration

My chakras are spinning in alignment

My aura is colorful and clutter-free

My light body beams brightly

I am centered and balanced

As you repeat the incantations, visualize them taking effect. Imagine them at work, balancing your chakras. For instance, when you say 'My heart is filled with love,' try to feel the heart chakra getting filled with love. It is important to make sure that you are not merely reading or repeating the incantations. The more you believe in them, the more you benefit from them. At the end of the exercise, if performed correctly, you will be able to feel the change.

Chapter 10. Chakra Exercises

Every healthy style of living includes exercises. They keep our body in balance, improve our flexibility, and prevent rigidity. When we work out, our body works hard and makes us forget about our petty issues. Instead of thinking about the past or the future, we find ourselves in the present. These physical activities improve our mood, help us de-stress, and leave us feeling good. Regular exercise also improves our sex life, keeps diseases at bay, and promotes sleep. When our chakras are not balanced, the quality of our sex life goes down, we find ourselves ill and easily get diseases and physical problems, and find it difficult to sleep. The chakra exercises, also known as chakracises, provide the same benefits as other exercises, but they also align, balance, and heal our chakras.

The following are the exercises for all the chakras:

The Root Chakra
You can balance, strengthen, and maintain your root chakra by:

- Doing squats
- Marching
- Stomping your feet

The Sacral Chakra

To balance, maintain, and heal your sacral chakra, you can perform the following two exercises:

- Pelvic thrusts
- Circular pelvis movements

The Solar Plexus Chakra

It can be aligned, healed, and balanced by the following exercises:

- Hula hooping
- Belly dancing
- Doing the twist

The Heart Chakra

The heart chakra can be fixed, healed, or harmonized by the following exercises:

- Hugging yourself
- Breaststroke swimming
- Push-ups

The Throat Chakra

The exercises for bringing the throat chakra into sync and harmony with the others, and for strengthening it, include:

- Singing
- Screaming
- Gargling with salt water

The Third Eye Chakra
Exercises for strengthening, enhancing, and improving the third eye chakra include:

- Remote viewing
- Lucid dreaming
- Visualization

The Crown Chakra
The crown chakra can be strengthened, balanced, and activated by performing the following exercises:

- Prayer
- Meditation

Aura Cleansing

All beings have an aura. Our auras are always around us, surrounding us, and they also pick up energies from around us. The kind of energy that is in our aura also affects us and our chakras, so it is important to have a healthy and clean aura that is free of all negative and harmful energies. When our aura is not in a healthy state, we get tired, fatigued, and are easily irritated or annoyed. Our breathing becomes shallow and we tend to feel cornered. When these signs are present, it is time for us to cleanse our aura.

We can cleanse our aura by taking an aura cleansing shower or bath. You can cleanse your aura and rid it of negative powers by doing the following:

- Take a shower

- Smudge with a sage wand
- Take deep cleaning breaths
- Add Epsom salt to the tub when bathing

For maximum effect it is highly recommended that you perform these exercises regularly. The exercises are very simple and easy to perform, do not take much time, and are not only good for your chakras, but also physically beneficial to your body. By regularly performing these exercises you can get into a routine which will ensure that your chakras stay aligned, and in balance and harmony throughout the week.

Chapter 11. Toning your Chakras with Sounds

An easy way to tone the chakras is by using sounds. It is perhaps the easiest way of balancing the chakras. Our voice is a blend of energies and energy breakers. When we speak, there are sounds our mouth produces that favor the chakras, and there are sounds we produce that go against them. So, to tone our chakras, we need to practice producing the right sounds. Vowels have the information energy in them, and consonants are the energy breakers. The vowels carry our intentions in them and that is why they are revered and sacred in Chinese, Egyptian, Hebrew, Arabic, Japanese, and Sanskrit. These sounds tend to resonate with our chakras. The vowels are also used in mantras to help increase concentration and focus; meditators use mantras to become one with themselves and the universe. The words in the Vedas, especially the Sanskrit words, are also used as mantras; they are called the Bija mantras, and are used to align the chakras. Sounds have psychoactive properties and they can alter and enhance our consciousness. While the sounds are powerful, they are also completely in our control; you can start and stop as you please. One of the reasons they are held sacred is because they are so natural and so personal at the same time.

How to Tone your Chakras with Sounds
To start toning your chakras with sound, first you need to find yourself a comfortable and peaceful environment. You can sit on the floor, on a cushion, or in a chair. Since the chakras are around the spine, and the spine also plays an important part in the flow of energy, try to keep your spine as straight as

possible. When making the sounds, try not to go out of your way or try too hard; instead, make the sounds in as natural a way as possible. It can be a bit difficult to do so in the beginning because we are not really used to hearing our own voices and it can be distracting, but with a few days of practice it will become natural and easy.

Here are the sounds for the seven major chakras:

The Root Chakra
Sound: UH - 'U' as in 'up'

Repeat: 7 times

The Sacral Chakra
Sound: OOO - 'O' as in 'oat'

Repeat: 7 times

The Solar Plexus Chakra
Sound: 'OH' - 'O' as in 'no'

Repeat: 7 times

The Heart Chakra
Sound: 'AH' - 'A' as in 'ma'

Repeat: 7 times

The Throat Chakra
Sound: 'EYE' - pronunciation rhymes with 'why'

Repeat: 7 times

The Third Eye Chakra
Sound: 'AYE' - pronunciation rhymes with 'day'

Repeat: 7 times

The Crown Chakra
Sound: 'EEE' - pronounced to rhyme with 'me'

Repeat: 7 times

The After Exercise

Once you have toned all of your major chakras, you need to relax and hold your position for at least 10 minutes. In these 10 minutes, the energy in your body will balance out. Sometimes, as a result of toning, you might get light-headed; in that case, intone 'OOH' and 'AAH' to fully restore your consciousness.

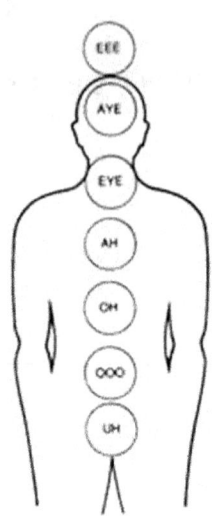

Chapter 12. Chakra Mudras

Mudras are special hand gestures that are used to open chakras. They are found in Hinduism and Buddhism. For opening the chakras with mudras, the techniques of mudras are combined with meditation. They also incorporate elements of visualization, colors, and sounds. Ideally, you should mix the mudras with the toning sounds mentioned in the previous chapter.

To begin, first get into a quiet environment and sit in a comfortable position. Slow down your breathing. Inhale through the nose and exhale through the mouth. Breathe slowly so that each inhalation and exhalation takes five seconds. After taking 10 slow breaths, you can move on to the mudras.

These are the mudras for all the chakras:

The First Chakra - Root
Bring the tip of your index finger to the tip of your thumb. Focusing on the spine where your root chakra is, visualize a red color, and intone 'LAM.' It rhymes with 'balm.'

The Second Chakra - Sacral
Join your hands and rest them in your lap with the palms facing upwards. The right hand should be on the top of the left hand, its palm over its fingers. Visualize the color orange, focus on the location of your sacral chakra, a little above the root, and feel the energy resonate inside you. Make the sound 'VAM.'

The Third Chakra - Solar Plexus
For this chakra you should place your hands on your stomach with the fingertips of both hands joined and pointing away from your stomach. Then focus on the navel area and visualize a yellow color. Chant 'RAM.'

The Fourth Chakra - Heart
For this chakra you need to sit with your legs crossed. Join the tip of your index finger with the tip of your thumb, like you did for the root chakra. Place your right hand right where your heart chakra is, and put your left hand on your knee. Then visualize a green color and chant 'YAM.'

The Fifth Chakra - Throat
Now, for the fifth chakra, you have to cross your fingers, but without the thumbs; the thumbs should be at the top while the fingers are crossed inside of the hands. Then visualize the color blue while focusing on your throat, and chant 'HAM.'

The Sixth Chakra - Third Eye
Begin by placing your hands a little below the breasts. Keep the middle fingers straight, pointing forward, and touching at the tops, while the other fingers are bent so only the two middle digits are touching. The thumbs should touch at the tops and point in your direction. Visualize the color indigo, focus on the middle of your forehead, and chant 'Om.'

The Seventh Chakra - Crown

Again, put your hands on your stomach with the ring fingers pointing upward and touching at the top. The other fingers should be crossed with the right thumb over the left thumb. Then visualize the color purple, focus on your crown or the top of your head, and chant 'NG.' The sound is deep and more in your mind than on the tip of your tongue.

As with the previous exercises, once you are finished, try not to get up immediately. Take time to take it all in, let the energies settle, and allow your body to prepare itself for the world. Getting up immediately would make you feel light-headed, but relaxing for 5-10 minutes after this exercise will prevent that. It also gives you a few minutes to reflect, relax, and cherish yourself.

Chapter 13. Aura

Aura is an energy that surrounds us. It is inside and outside our body. It acts like a magnet and attracts other energies too, both positive and negative. Psychics are often able to see and tell the color of people's auras. All beings, humans and animals, living and non-living, have an aura. If the aura is strong, it can protect us from the negative energies by acting as a shield. Every aura has multiple layers, including emotional, physical, and spiritual. The basic colors of the auras are the same as the colors of the chakras, the seven rainbow colors. The colors change as we change emotionally and spiritually. Our auras reflect our environment, our thinking, our outlook, our experiences, etc. Anyone who can see auras can tell a lot about a person just by looking at their aura. If we know the colors of our auras we can learn a great deal about ourselves too.

Here's a list of aura colors and what they mean:

Red
A red aura is found on energetic individuals and enthusiasts. People who are adventurous, like to travel, and are bold also have red auras. They are short-tempered and can get irritated easily, but they are also benevolent.

Yellow
A yellow aura is associated with intellectuals. They are intelligent, logical, and think analytically. They are hard-working and love their work more than anything else. They are

generally content on their own and do not need company of others, but can also get depressed or stressed.

Pink
It is associated with loving and caring people. They are social, friendly, love, and are loved. They are faithful, romantic, loyal, and also eat healthy and take good care of their bodies.

Green
A green aura is found on creative people. Perfectionists, realists, hard workers, etc. also have a green aura. They have various hobbies and like to cook, garden, decorate, etc. They have a great aesthetic sense, cherish beauty, and tend to be very pragmatic.

Orange
People with an orange aura are generous and social. They also do well in the company of others, whether they are the life of the party or not. They are honest, kind, sympathetic, and empathic. They have a natural charm about them and are easy to be around.

Purple
The purple aura is found on psychics or people who are too emotional. They also have a very mysterious air about them. They are keen and like to explore and learn whatever they can. They have an inherent thirst for knowledge and are generally interesting.

Blue

Leaders usually have a blue aura. It is chiefly associated with people who are charismatic, eloquent, and can communicate well. They find it easy to express themselves through their words and in various forms of art.

Gold

Artists are mainly associated with a gold aura. They have a taste for fine things, enjoy decorations and beauty, appreciate anything that is exquisite, and thrive when they are at the center of attention. They also make good entertainers.

Silver / White

Anyone with a silver or white aura is very gifted and wise. They also have psychic abilities, a good intuition, and are sensitive. They do well as mentors and counsellors. It is easy for them to relate to people on a spiritual level.

Black

Negative people have a black aura. People with mental illnesses like depression have it, and so do people who are full of hatred and misery.

Chapter 14. Chakras in Hinduism and Buddhism

Hinduism
Since this has already been discussed in detail in the beginning, I will keep this one brief. Chakras have their roots in the Vedas, and are linked to yoga. The chants, mudras, and incantations of the chakras can be used while doing yoga. In the Vedas, the chakras and yoga meditations have often been mentioned together. The Sanskrit word 'kundalin' means 'she who lies coiled,' and is used in chakras to refer to a snake lying coiled between the anus and the genitals, a nod to the power of the serpent.

In Tantra and Yoga, the seven chakras are:

- Muladhara
- Swadhisthana
- Manipura
- Anahata
- Vishuddi
- Agya
- Sahasrara

Buddhism
When studying Hinduism and Buddhism, we often find them overlapping at several points. Meditations, yoga, mantra, etc., are found in both Hinduism and Buddhism. Tantric practices are also found in Tibetan Buddhism. The chakras in Buddhism have varying meanings and representations, and they are:

- Crown - Spiritual
- Third Eye - Perception
- Throat - Expression
- Heart - Love
- Solar Plexus - Power
- Sacral - Sex
- Root - Survival

The Differences between Hinduism and Buddhism Relating to Chakras

In Hinduism there are seven major chakras, but in Buddhism there are 4 -10 major chakras. In Buddhism, the solar plexus chakra is mapped lower than it is mapped in Hinduism. We also see that the energy is usually visualized as moving upwards, from root to the head, in Hinduism, but in Buddhism, the case is opposite, and the energy is visualized as travelling down from the crown, often to the heart.

But, whatever the key differences, there are many similarities, and we can all agree upon their benefits.

Chapter 15. Opening the Chakras and Meditation

As you go through this book you will realize how important it is for your chakras to be open. It is harmful to have your chakras in a blocked, inactive, underactive or even overactive state. Fortunately, when you open your chakras this problem is pretty much solved. This is because problems occur when some chakras are closed and the others try to make up for this void.

Identifying and fixing a chakra imbalance can make a very big and positive difference in a person's life. Quite a bit of the information in this book is here is to help you do exactly that. All the various exercises are to help you open your chakras and keep them in balance. Only then can you keep yourself in a positive state both mentally and physically.

I will now tell you some more about how you can open each chakra and attain this state of chakra balance. You will also see how meditation makes an immense difference in this.

Let us discuss chakra meditation. It is something that will help you so extensively that I'm sure you will continue this practice for a long time. There are many experts who can guide you to do it properly and get the maximum benefit from each meditative session.

First find a place where you can focus on the task at hand without any extra distractions. You should be able to relax in this place without having to deal with external sounds, other people, etc.

Then sit in the proper position, with your back straight so that your weight is balanced at the center. As with any type of meditation, focus on your breathing. Get a proper balance as you inhale and exhale for equal beats of time. It should be a relaxing rhythm that helps you feel completely calm and increases your focus.

Now follow the steps with respect to each chakra as given below. The whole practice should usually be done within 30 minutes at most, so it is something everyone can find time for.

The Root Chakra

- If your root chakra is working overtime you will probably be more concerned with materialistic matters. If it is not working enough, feelings of fear and anxiety are more prominent. There might also be a problem with feeling insecure and always being scared of life. To open this chakra, regularly strengthen your body through some form of movement, like a walk or short jog done every morning.
- Another way to open your root chakra is as follows. First relax your body and stand straight. Keep your feet a little apart, at about shoulder-width distance, and bend your knees a bit as you thrust your lower body slightly forward. Stay like this for a while. This gets you in a grounded state before you start to meditate. Then sit on the ground in a cross-legged position with each hand extended and resting on the knee. Keep the fingers open, other than the thumb and index, which should be touching each other. Now concentrate on the position of your root chakra. Be relaxed and start chanting the "LAM" sound. As you do this, get completely relaxed and then visualize a petaled flower, which represents energy, opening. Take in a deep breath and release it. You will feel much better and

realize the difference. You can do this in the mornings, when your body will be fresh, and it will be best for you to do it in an open space.
- You can also make use of certain colors and stones to help attain relief from the blockage of the root chakra, which is connected to the color red and is an earth chakra. The stone best suited to cleanse this chakra is a red garnet or jasper. These can be worn on the body in some form like a ring or chain.

The Sacral Chakra
- When this chakra is underactive, you will be more introverted and hesitant about opening up to others. On the other hand, when it is overactive, instead of being unemotional, you will be hypersensitive. You will have problems with confidence and low self-worth. You might also feel intimidated by others. This chakra is also closest to the pubis, so a blockage here can mean that you are going to have problems with your sexuality and a lot of inhibitions about your body. You will not feel confident and have problems with a partner.
- To open this chakra, kneel down, keeping your back in a straight yet relaxed position. Extend your hands over your lap and place one on top of the other, keeping the palms facing up. The thumbs should stay in contact. Then concentrate on the position of the sacral chakra and start chanting the "VAM" sound. Relax and reflect on what this chakra stands for till you feel a sort of cleansing feeling. Again, it is best that you perform this early in the morning as it can help you make the most of your energy.

- This chakra is associated with the color orange and is said to be a water chakra. You can cleanse it using a tiger's eye or an orange calcite.

The Navel Chakra

- When this chakra is underactive you will not be confident and will give in to others easily, as you won't trust your own decisions. You will suffer from low self-esteem and self-worth. You will turn into an introvert when this chakra has blockages. You might also develop depression as a result, which might cause you to shut the world out. However, when it is overacting you get too aggressive and overconfident. You will develop an unnecessarily large ego and be an extrovert. You might also feel overwhelmed at times.
- For this chakra, stand with your back straight yet relaxed and lower yourself onto your knees like you did above. Then bend your elbows so that your hands are placed in front of your stomach. The palms should touch each other with all the fingers straight, other than the thumbs, which should cross over each other. Now concentrate on the position of the navel chakra and all that it is related to. Relax and chant the "RAM" sound till you feel completely calm. You can do this in early afternoon or early morning.
- This chakra is associated with the color yellow, and you can make use of a yellow calcite or citrine.

The Heart Chakra

- This one is closest to the heart and so it deals with love and affection. If it is in an underactive state, you are unapproachable and unfriendly towards others. You will have problems in giving and receiving love. You will not be able to express your love freely. In an overactive state your expression of love is exaggerated to the level that people feel suffocated. You may not mean to, but you end up over-expressing yourself and possibly driving the other person away.
- For this chakra, sit in a cross-legged position. Keep the fingers of each hand open, other than the thumb and index finger, which should be touching. Place your right hand on your chest in a lower central position. Keep your left hand over your left knee with the palm facing up. Now concentrate on the position of the heart chakra and think about all that it entails. Start chanting the "YAM" sound in a clear manner. Continue to do this till you feel completely calm and your body feels cleansed.
- This chakra is associated with the color green and the element of air, and the stone best suited to cleanse this chakra is jade. You can wear an arm bracelet or a pendant that hangs over the heart.

The Throat Chakra

- In an underactive state your throat chakra will cause shy behavior. Blockages in your throat chakra can also cause throat problems, such as sore throat, and speech problems so that you will have a hard time speaking. There might also be problems with creativity, and people with a blockage here might develop hearing problems as well. In an overactive state the throat chakra leads you to talk incessantly at an annoying rate.

People do not have control over their speech and thoughts, which is often annoying to others. Sufferers may say things that don't make sense or lack imagination and creativity.
- Here you should again lower yourself onto your knees and sit. Your hands should be in the appropriate mudra for this chakra and in a position in front of your throat chakra. Concentrate on the position of your chakra and chant the "HAM" sound clearly. As you do this, think about the functions of this particular chakra and how you want it to affect your life. Keep doing this till you feel totally relaxed and cleansed again.
- This chakra is associated with the color blue and the element ether.

The Third Eye Chakra
- In an underactive state, this chakra causes people to rely on others' beliefs and decisions. A kind of overdependence can occur, and the person might not be able to take independent decisions about work and personal matters. In an overactive state, the third eye chakra could make you an avid daydreamer who is out of touch with reality. That is mainly because it promotes a very active subconscious, which will allow you to believe anything that your subconscious mind thinks to be true. With a severely overactive sixth chakra, a person might even have hallucinations and see or hear things that are not present.
- First sit down in a cross-legged position and then place your hands before you in front of the lower part of the chest. Take up the appropriate mudra mentioned above for this chakra. Now focus on the position of the chakra and start chanting the "OM" sound clearly. As you do

this, think about all that this chakra represents in your life. Continue this till you are relaxed completely and once again experience that cleansed feeling flowing through your body. You can do this in the mornings.
- This chakra is associated with the color indigo or blue. The stone best suited for this chakra is amethyst.

The Crown Chakra

- In an underactive state, this chakra will cause you to be very rigid and not as connected to the spiritual world. You will not be satisfied with anything and have problems with the smallest of things. Nothing will satisfy you and you will want all sorts of worldly things. It might also cause headaches and decision-making difficulties. In an overactive state it will cause you to over-think everything and you will take your spiritual devotion to an extreme level. You will start to feel like you have direct access to God and that you can speak to him personally. You will also try and force your philosophies on others and try to make them think like you.
- Once again, you should sit in a cross-legged position and place your hands in front of your stomach. Take up the appropriate mudra for the crown chakra and keep your back straight. Concentrate on the position of the crown chakra and start chanting the "NG" sound in a clear manner. As you do this, reflect over what this chakra is concerned with and how you want it to affect your life. Keep it going till you are fully relaxed and peaceful. This chakra requires more time and should be dealt with after all the other chakras are in a proper state. You can do this early in the mornings.

- This chakra is associated with the color violet, and the stone best suited for it is quartz.

One effective meditation practice is visualizing light passing through each chakra during meditation. Visualize a flow of white light through your chakras in a motion similar to that of a liquid. It will be as though each chakra is an empty gateway that allows this fluid white light to enter. As you focus on each chakra you will know when to move on to the next as that particular chakra will start to feel warm.

Finally, the ball of light collects all the blockages and exits your system through the top of your head.

Grounding yourself during meditation is also important. This means that you try to feel as connected as possible to the earth beneath you. This is usually done by imagining yourself with roots growing beneath you. These roots should extend and firmly attach themselves to the ground below just like those of a large tree.

Practicing meditation daily will help you get better at it, and soon you will do it as a habitual exercise. Doing this once or twice is not going to make any difference. It has to be done over a month or two to see any substantial results.

Over a period of time you will start to notice the difference as your chakras open up and attain a good balance. Continuing the meditation will then help you maintain this balanced state that you have attained after so much effort.

Chapter 16. Chakras in Relationship

As we have seen, chakras influence so many different aspects of our lives, from our own bodies to our relation with the external world. This relationship could be with our family, friends, lovers or the universe at large. And we all know that these relationships are an important part of our lives.

However, most people struggle to find a good balance in relationships, and everyone has problems at some point. Chakras make a difference in this too. Imbalance in your chakras could be the reason behind quite a few relationship problems, if not all; finding that balance can also solve them. It may be that the chakras in your body – or the other person's – are underactive, overactive or even completely blocked.

I will now explain how these problems manifest in you and cause problems with other people.

- Due to the root chakra you might feel an extensive negativity towards people and also doubt if you will find a good life partner. This chakra could cause you to think too much about yourself and how to survive without getting hurt.
- The sacral chakra will let you be easily affected by the energy of the people around you, and this can have quite a negative impact.
- The solar plexus chakra could be why you don't make active efforts in your relationships with other people. You may be lost in daydreams without making a real effort to make these dreams come true.
- The heart chakra is usually what makes love easier, but otherwise it can cause you to feel negative emotions like

jealousy and loneliness. You will be so absorbed in yourself that you feel insecure and abandoned.
- The throat chakra could also make you feel insecure about yourself. This is hard on other people as well, as they can't make you feel good when you don't feel that way about yourself. You will be too worried about external appearances and self-conscious about everything that you do.
- The third eye chakra can make you very moody and emotionally unstable. This really does not do any good in relationships, as you're likely to take things the wrong way. The emotional upheavals will also leave you exhausted.
- The crown chakra could be why you are rigid in your thoughts and unwilling to pay heed to the opinions of others. You will tend to be more confused about things and also face trust issues.

As you can see, if the chakras are not in an open and balanced state, they can cause many issues which affect your relationships. All these negative manifestations will hinder you from having a positive and healthy relationship with anyone. When such issues are in the way, it is not possible to interact or communicate with the other person you care about. Of course, they may be facing such issues as well. Use all the information I have provided to find a balanced state for your chakras. Once you do this, you will see so many positive manifestations in your life and relationships.

In such a positive state, the chakras will give you positive results as well:

- The root chakra will help you to be more grounded and calm. This will help you keep a more optimistic outlook towards relationships and keep a positive balance.

- The sacral chakra will be more controlled and won't take in negative energy as easily as it used to. This will help you be in a more positive state and accept positive energy only. Intercourse is a better experience with the help of this chakra.
- The solar plexus chakra keeps you in a more balanced state. This makes you positive and encourages you to make active efforts towards your relationships. This will give good vibes to other people as well as making you seem more approachable.
- The heart chakra is what helps make loving easier. You will feel better about yourself and be more willing to see the good in others. This chakra helps in the exchange of love from both sides.
- The throat chakra gives you more confidence about yourself and helps you keep a positive state of mind. Being confident from the inside will reflect on the outside and make you more attractive to other people as well. You won't have senseless insecurities about your appearance anymore.
- The third eye chakra will help keep negative energy at bay and push you in a better direction in all aspects of your life. This will help you be more positive in expecting the good things in life instead of being negative all the time.
- The crown chakra will help hone your spiritual instincts. Positive energy will circulate a lot more and you will be more forgiving as well as humble. This will make the other person appreciate your efforts and make solving any arguments much quicker as well.

All these chakras will make your life with others a much better experience when they are in a balanced state.

Conclusion

Here, I conclude this book. The chakras are very powerful, immense, and intricate. Instead of running you quickly through all the chakras, I focused on the major chakras in this book. The major chakras are more powerful and important, and if you have them aligned and balanced then the minor chakras automatically fall into place.

By the time most people realize the existence and power of chakras, they find that their chakras are out of balance, not aligned properly, and damaged, but that is nothing to worry about because they can be re-aligned, healed, and balanced easily, as you have already discovered in this book. The chakras affect us on almost every level, which means that we should not ignore them if we want peace and happiness in our lives. And, at the same time, it also makes it easier for us to correct them because there are all the more ways to do so. These include exercises, chants, incantations, gems, stones, color therapy, etc., all of which are already explained in this book.

The chakras may be difficult for some people to understand, but in this book, I have kept things as simple as possible, without missing anything important. Instead of clouding your mind and confusing you with heaps of information, I chose to stick to the main points so that you can grasp the concepts easily. You will find this book to be informative and practical at the same time, so whether you wanted a refresher to clarify your understanding or wanted to jump straight in and activate or balance your chakras, you won't find yourself searching for answers and will be able to start right away.

I hope you find this book useful and helpful.

Thank you.

Key Takeaways from This Book

- There are seven major chakras.
- The chakras are energy centers that gather, distribute, and balance the energies in our body.
- Each chakra has a specific location in our body.
- Each chakra controls and governs a part of our being.
- A chakra that is not balanced results in physical, mental, and emotional diseases, issues, and problems.
- There are several ways to activate, align, balance, and harmonize your chakras, including chants, incantations, exercises, and therapies.
- It is important to balance the chakras to lead a happy, healthy, and a successful life.

How to Put This Information into Action

To make the most of this book, I recommend the following steps:

1. First, you should learn about the chakras to understand what they are, where they are, and what they do.
2. Second, you need to identify what state your chakras are in. Are they balanced or unbalanced? Aligned or not? Underactive or overactive? Blocked or open?
3. Then work on fixing them. All the necessary exercises for activating, balancing, and aligning them can be found in this book, so you can start right away!

Resources for Further Reading

Websites

Chakra Energy Training: http://www.chakratraining.com

Chakra Blog: http://chakradiaries.wordpress.com

Chakra 101: http://www.yogajournal.com/yoga-101/a-guide-to-the-chakras/

Significance of the Major Chakras: http://sadhguru.org/atoz/c/seven-chakras-significance/

Books

Anatomy of the Spirit: The Seven Stages of Power and Healing by Caroline Myss

Chakra Clearing by Doreen Virtue

Wheels of Life: A User's Guide to the Chakra System by Anodea Judith

Eastern Body, Western Mind: Psychology and the Chakra System as a Path to the Self by Anodea Judith

Preview of Essential Oils: Learn How to Use the Power of Essential Oils for Aromatherapy, Weight Loss, Stress Relief and Beauty

Chapter 9. Essential Oils and Aromatherapy

Your sense of smell can be extraordinarily provocative. From fresh cut grass and lavender, to homemade pizza and cinnamon doughnuts, our sense of smell can take us from one room to another. How many times have you walked passed a restaurant and thought 'Oh, I must come back and try their food.'

The Power of Scent

Did you know that we can distinguish around 10,000 different smells? It is easy to see why such a powerful tool can be used to help decide what smells are good for us or make as happy.

When inhaled, aromas can stimulate brain function incredibly quickly. This is why aromatherapy oils are such a pleasant way for us to treat skin complaints or just lighten our mood. It is generally accepted that a new smell can change our moods. It is not just about the pleasant smell; inhaled properties can be fed rapidly into the bloodstream thereby affecting our moods.

The full potential of these healing properties are not yet fully realized, but we do know that many of the variety of applications are not just for pain relief or mood enhancers.

They also lend to increase cognitive function and boost energy levels.

Aromatherapy

- ✓ Stress relief and relaxation benefits
- ✓ Mood calming, inner balance and harmony
- ✓ Relief of discomfort
- ✓ Boost benefits for the immune and circulatory systems

Go ahead, light a scented candle and let the aroma of these essential oils do its work.

Emotion	Aroma
Aggression	Rosemary, Ylang-ylang, Bergamot, Chamomile, Juniper, Lemon
Anger	Palma Rosa, Rose, Rosemary, Ylang-Ylang, Chamomile, Jasmine, Marjoram
Anxiety	Rose (for confidence), Sandalwood. Sweet Marjoram, Vetiver (for grounding) Neroli, Bergamot, Chamomile, Frankincense, Geranium (for balance), Lavender, Orange, Patchouli,
Disappointment	Rose, Bergamot, Cypress, Frankincense, Jasmine, Orange
Fear	Fennel, Ginger, Patchouli, Sandalwood, Thyme, Cedarwood
Grief	Jasmine, Marjoram, Neroli, Rose, Chamomile, Bergamot
Hysteria	Neroli, Orange, Lavender, Tea Tree, Chamomile
Impatience	Chamomile, Lavender, Frankincense
Indecision	Peppermint, Patchouli, Basil, Clary, Cypress,

	Jasmine
Jealousy	Rose, Jasmine
Loneliness	Marjoram
Fatigue (emotional and mental	Peppermint, Rosemary, Thyme, Basil, Clary, Cardamon, Cinnamon leaf or bark, Ginger, Grapefruit, Orange, Palmarosa, Ylang-ylang
Fatigue (physical)	Peppermint, Rosemary, Lavender, Ginger, Lemon, Basil
Nervousness	Frankincense, Orange, Chamomile, Coriander, Vetiver
Panic	Chamomile, Jasmine, Ylang-ylang, Lavender
Sadness	Jasmine, Rose, Rosewood
Shock	Tea tree, Lavender, Rose, Neroli
Shyness	Ginger, Jasmine, Patchouli, Peppermint, Ylang-ylang
Stress	Lavender, Sweet Marjoram, Chamomile, Frankincense, Sandalwood, Ylang-ylang, Rosemary and all Citrus oils
Suspicion	Lavender, Jasmine
Tension	Ylang-ylang, Sandalwood, Orange, Rose, Rosewood, Lavender, Chamomile, Frankincense, Jasmine, Geranium

Essential Oils to Avoid

Just like certain plants, you should be wary of essential oils that might prove counterproductive when it comes in contact to the skin, or when it is ingested. Some of these essential oils can cause allergic reactions and may even be poisonous.

The oils on the list below are best avoided:

- Calamus
- Horseradish
- Tansy
- Savin
- Rue
- Southernwood
- Yellow camphor
- Mustard
- Bitter almond
- Mugwort

Tip: Do not use the same essential oil exclusively over a long period of time as you may develop sensitivity to the oil.

To download the rest of this book, please click on the following link:

http://www.amazon.com/gp/product/B00LDEM0HI

More Books You Might Like

Household DIY: Save Time and Money with Do It Yourself Hints and Tips on Furniture, Clothes, Pests, Stains, Residues, Odors and More!

DIY Household Hacks: Save Time and Money with Do It Yourself Tips and Tricks for Cleaning Your House

Essential Oils: Essential Oils & Aromatherapy for Beginners: Proven Secrets to Weight Loss, Skin Care, Hair Care & Stress Relief Using Essential Oil Recipes

Apple Cider Vinegar for Beginners: An Apple Cider Vinegar Handbook with Proven Secrets to Natural Weight Loss, Optimum Health and Beautiful Skin

Body Butter Recipes: Proven Formula Secrets to Making All Natural Body Butters that Will Hydrate and Rejuvenate Your Skin

If the links do not work, for whatever reason, you can simply search for these titles on the Amazon website to find them.

Your Free Bonus

As a way of thanking you for your purchase, I'm offering you an opportunity to sign up and be a part of an exclusive book list where members get advanced notice on high-quality books.

To be part of this exclusive club, click on the link below:

https://docs.google.com/forms/d/1ttDqtdRjOeAEtA-BKnq5Hw668vjQSoVWcXCGQ8z9frA/viewform

www.ingramcontent.com/pod-product-compliance
Lightning Source LLC
Chambersburg PA
CBHW071422070526
44578CB00003B/659